MANLY BOOK

OF

EXPERIENCES

DESERET
BOOK

SALT LAKE CITY, UTAH

To family members, friends, or others who read this:
The following pages are recorded to prove to future
generations that I was indeed a manly man.

X _____

Contents

1. Manly Injuries:
Stitches, Broken Bones, and Lacerations

2. Daring Stunts I've Tried

3. Moments of Manly Courage and Bravery

4. Times I've Shed a Manly Tear

(No, this is not one of them.)

5. Hard Things I've Overcome

6. My Sports Achievements, Victories, and Records

6

7. Favorite Athletes and Sports Teams

8. How I Stay in Peak Physical Condition

9. Physical Attributes, Strengths, and Abilities

10. Outdoor Adventures:
Climbing, Hiking, Camping

11. Animals I've Hunted and Fish I've Caught

12. My Favorite Scouting Memories

12

13. Places I've Traveled To

14. Places I've Lived

15. My Favorite Foods and Restaurants and Exotic Things I've Eaten

16. Unbelievable and Amazing Things I've Seen

17. Spiritual Experiences I've Had

18. Service I've Given

18

19. Times My Prayers Have Been Answered

20. The First People I Want to See When I Get to Heaven

21. My Favorite Scripture Verses and Stories

22. Prophets and Apostles Who Inspire Me

22

23. Memories from General Conference and Priesthood Session

24. How the Gospel Has Made Me a Better Man

25. My Feelings about Jesus Christ, the Perfect Man

25

26. What I've Learned (or Hope to Learn) from My Mission

27. Books That Have Influenced My Life

28. My Favorite Movies and Music

29. Things I Want to Create

30. Stuff I've Fixed and Stuff I've Broken

31. My Skills and Hobbies

32. My Goals and Ambitions

33. Accomplishments I'm Most Proud Of

35. When I've Been a Leader

35

36. Jobs I've Had and Money I've Earned

37. Memorable Dates I've Been On

37

38. Deep Thoughts on Politics and Religion

39. Man's Best Friends
(Pets I've Had)

40. My Manly Friends and Buddies

41. Men I Respect

41

42. Women I Respect

42

43. Cool Family Traditions

44. Lessons I've Learned from My Brother (What to Do and What *Not* to Do)

45. Times I've Protected My Sister (and Times *She's* Protected Me)

46. Things I've Learned from My Mother

47. Qualities I Admire in My Father

47

48. Memories I Have of My Grandparents

48

49. Things I'll Never Forget

50. Advice I Would Give the Next Generation

More Manly Experiences...

52

54

55

56

58

63

64

82

84